EVERYDAY SCIENCE

Turning Up the Heat:
Energy

Ann Fullick

Heinemann
LIBRARY
Chicago, Illinois

© 2005 Heinemann Library
Published by Heinemann Library,
A division of Reed Elsevier, Inc.
Chicago, IL

For information, address the publisher:
Heinemann Library, 100 N. LaSalle, Suite 1200, Chicago, IL 60602
Customer Service: 888-363-4266
Visit our website at www.heinemannlibrary.com

Printed and bound in China by South China Printing Company.
08 07 06 05 04
10 9 8 7 6 5 4 3 2 1

Library of Congress Cataloging-in-Publication Data
Fullick, Ann, 1956-
   Turning up the heat : energy / Ann Fullick.
      p. cm. -- (Everyday science)
Summary: An overview of what energy is and how it is generated and used, describing different types of energy, ways to measure and renew energy resources, and energy for the future.
Includes bibliographical references and index.
   ISBN 1-4034-4817-5 (HC), 1-4034-6423-5 (PB)
   1. Force and energy--Juvenile literature. 2. Power
resources--Juvenile literature. [1. Force and energy. 2. Power
resources.] I. Title. II. Everyday science (Heinemann Library (Firm))
   QC73.4.F84 2004
   531'.6--dc22

                              2003014850

Acknowledgments
The publishers would like to thank the following for permission to reproduce photographs: Action Plus p.15; Anthony Blake p.25; CORBIS/Ressmeyer pp.40, 48; Fraser p.12; Getty pp.4, 9, 13, 16, 24, 37; NASA p.32; Photodisc pp.5, 19, 20, 36, 47; Photodisc/Getty p.31; SPL pp.10, 49; SPL/Science Industry & Business Library p.34; SPL/Frieder p.42; SPL/Hart-Davis p.30; SPL/Pasieka p.38; SPL/Sheila Terry p.35; SPL/Sher p.23; SPL/Syred p.41; SPL/TRL Ltd p.14; Steve Behr p.6; Still Pictures/Schytte p.50; Team Green/Shell p.52.

Cover photograph of runners crossing a finishing line reproduced by permission of Corbis.

Artwork by Ascenders apart from Jeff Edwards p.29; Mark Franklin pp.17, 33.

The publishers would like to thank Robert Snedden for his assistance in the preparation of this book.

Contents

Energy Everywhere

Wherever you are, whatever you are doing, energy is sure to be involved. You use lighting when it gets dark, heating when it gets cold, and hot water for washing. You ride in cars and maybe trains or buses. You listen to the radio and the CD player. Sometimes you watch television. You move around the house and you eat food. All of these things require energy.

What is energy?

We often talk about energy: "You have a lot of energy today." "A well-balanced meal gives you energy." "Using energy-efficient appliances saves money." "Don't waste energy." Saying the word is one thing, but saying exactly what we mean by it is a

Plenty going on
Study this picture and see how many different uses of energy you can spot.

different matter. Energy can be roughly defined as what is needed for any activity to take place.

Energy varieties

The universe is full of energy. Much of it is what we call low-grade energy—that is, it is not useful because it is so spread out. The energy we can use every day is concentrated energy. Concentrated energy comes in different forms, such as electrical energy, light energy, sound energy, and heat energy. Kinetic energy, potential energy, and chemical energy are also essential parts of our everyday lives.

Fierce but friendly
We transfer the chemical energy stored in logs into heat energy to warm us.

One exciting fact about energy is that it cannot be created or destroyed. It is simply changed from one form into another. When you turn on a light switch, the electrical energy traveling through the wires is changed into the light energy you see in the light bulb and the heat energy you feel coming off it. In the same way, the chemical energy in the food you eat is changed into heat energy, kinetic energy, and more chemical energy in the chemicals making up the cells of your body. Most energy ends up as part of the spread-out, low-grade energy filling the universe.

Using energy carefully

Energy is everywhere we look, from the spectacular lightning bolt to the slow all-day, everyday release of energy in our bodies that keeps us alive. Energy works for us all the time, but its misuse causes real problems. Chemical energy in the form of bombs and missiles causes death and destruction. Wildfires can destroy huge areas of countryside. Our use of fossil fuels has led, partly at least, to global climate changes. These are all part of the energy picture. We must use our energy resources carefully and responsibly to get the most out of them, while doing as little harm as possible to our world.

Measuring Energy

Because energy comes in so many different forms, we use different types of instruments to measure it and its effects. Can you remember the last time you were really sick? Someone probably felt your forehead to see if you were running a temperature, a sure sign that your body is fighting an infection. A transfer of heat energy raises the temperature of an object, whether it is a pot of water or your body. Your skin is very sensitive to changes in temperature, but touching something gives only a rough indication of how hot it is. To accurately measure temperature, or a change in temperature, we use an instrument called a thermometer.

How does a thermometer work?

The mercury bulb thermometer works on the principle that as liquids get hotter their volume increases (they expand), and when they cool their volume decreases (they contract).

Hot or cold?
The temperatures of household items vary a lot. It is sometimes useful to be able to measure them.

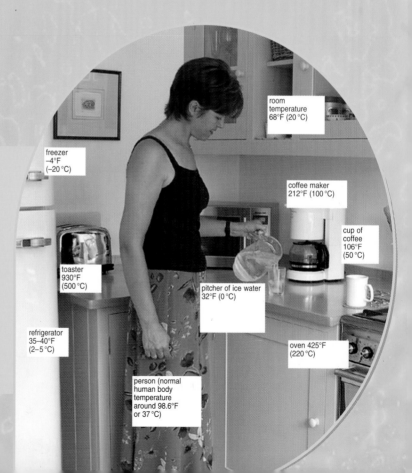

room temperature 68°F (20 °C)

freezer −4°F (−20 °C)

coffee maker 212°F (100 °C)

cup of coffee 106°F (50 °C)

toaster 930°F (500 °C)

pitcher of ice water 32°F (0 °C)

refrigerator 35–40°F (2–5 °C)

oven 425°F (220 °C)

person (normal human body temperature around 98.6°F or 37 °C)

A mercury thermometer has a bulb containing liquid mercury with a very narrow tube leading out of it. When the bulb is placed in a warm liquid, the mercury heats up, expands, and rises up the tube. The hotter the substance, the more the mercury expands and the farther its level in the tube rises. The thermometer has been calibrated so that certain levels of mercury stand for certain temperatures. The same principle is used in thermometers that measure outdoor or indoor temperatures. But in these thermometers, alcohol is used instead of mercury.

More ways of measuring temperature

In our homes are many places where we need to control the temperature, such as in ovens, refrigerators, freezers, and heating systems. For example, for cooking we need to put energy into the oven until it reaches a certain temperature, and when the food has cooked we need to turn off the energy until the temperature falls, or the food will burn. This system involves a thermostat. At the heart of a thermostat there is often a bimetallic strip—two metals joined together. One metal expands more than the other when it heats, and this makes the strip bend. In an oven the strip bends so that at a given temperature an electrical circuit is broken. This either directly cuts off the electricity heating the oven or reduces the flow of gas into the oven by narrowing the opening of a valve in the gas supply. Then, as the strip cools down and straightens, the contact is renewed and the oven heats up again. In refrigerators the opposite happens. The strip completes an electrical circuit as the temperature rises, then electrical energy is used to cool the contents of the refrigerator again.

Temperature-sensitive materials that change color at different temperatures can also be useful. They can be used for serious purposes, such as the fever strips used to check the temperature of very young children. Or they can be just for fun, like the mood rings people wear.

More Energy Measuring

Food contains the energy we need for life. Look on any food packaging and you will see a list of ingredients. Such lists usually include the energy content of the food, shown in calories.

Measuring food's energy

The amount of energy contained in a food can be found using a process known as calorimetry. An accurately weighed amount of the food is burned in pure oxygen. The heat given off is used to heat a known volume of water in a device called a calorimeter. The temperature of the water before and after heating is measured, and the change in temperature can be used to figure out how much heat energy was produced by burning the food. Next time you look at the energy content of your food, just imagine all the burning and measuring that has taken place to give you that information!

Measuring electricity

Electrical energy is needed for almost all the machines and gadgets we use. The television, washing machine, dishwasher, and computer all need electricity. Stores, offices, hospitals, and factories rely on a constant supply of electrical energy. When we measure electrical energy, several things have to be taken into account. Most important, the amount of electrical energy that an appliance transfers into heat, light, or whatever else is required will depend on two factors. The first is how long the appliance is switched on for. The second is how much electrical energy it can transfer in a given time (its power). Power is measured in watts (W) or kilowatts (kW). One kilowatt equals 1,000 watts. Power for small appliances such as hairdriers is measured in watts, but many bigger appliances transfer energy at a rate best measured in kilowatts. The amount of electricity we use in our homes is measured using a meter.

Energy units

The basic energy unit is the joule, named after 19th-century British scientist James Prescott Joule. Energy units used to be called calories, and food energy values are often given in calories and joules. Scientists use joules, but most people still use calories. It takes 4.2 joules of heat energy to raise the temperature of 1 gram of water by $1°C$ (4.2 joules = 1 calorie). Confusingly, the calories used to measure food are really kilocalories (C)—each equal to 1,000 calories.

Lighting-up time
Light meters are used in switches for street lights.
When the light level drops below a certain point,
the light is automatically switched on.

Measuring light energy

Light energy is a constant part of our lives. It enables us to see and provides energy for all the plants in the world to make their food. There are various ways of measuring light energy. They often involve a light meter. A light meter samples the light intensity over a given area and determines the average light intensity there. Light meters built into cameras make sure exactly the right amount of light reaches the film to take the best possible picture. Light meters also play an important part in some sports. In cricket, a bat-and-ball game popular in England, Australia, India, and some other countries, the umpires use light meters to decide if there is enough light for play to continue safely. If not, the game is stopped.

Living Sensors

Energy is vital to our existence, and our bodies are well-tuned energy-sensing machines. We see because our eyes are sensitive to light energy. They respond to changes in light intensity, or strength, by changing the amount of light that they let into the delicate light-sensitive cells at the back of the eyeball.

Light-sensitive eyes

You can see this working for yourself. Look closely at the pupils of your eyes in a well-lit mirror. They will look fairly small because the light intensity is high and so your eyes respond by limiting the amount of light that gets in. Now cover your eyes with your hands for a minute or so. Keep your eyes open. You are lowering the intensity of the light that reaches your eyes. Move your hands away quickly and watch carefully what happens to your pupils. They should be much wider open after being in the dark, to let more light in. But then you should see them shrink down again as you expose your eyes to bright light again.

Plants and light

Plants use light energy from the Sun to make sugar from carbon dioxide and water in a process called photosynthesis. They change the direction of their leaves throughout the day to soak up as much light as possible. Plants growing in shade will grow upward extra fast, hurrying to capture more light energy from the Sun. If they cannot reach sunlight, many plants grow bigger leaves to catch more light energy.

Sound-sensitive ears

You are sensitive to sound energy, too. Your ears pick up sounds over quite a wide range, but they cannot hear sounds at the extremes of the range. Other animals are far more sensitive to sound energy than we are. Dogs can hear whistles that we cannot because they are sensitive to high-pitched sounds that our ears cannot pick up. Bats use sound energy to fly in dim light and to detect their insect prey.

Guardian cells

Your skin contains nerve cells, shown here in orange, that pick up and measure heat energy. The nerve cells carry information around our bodies.

Heat-sensitive skin

Human skin is very sensitive to temperature differences. Although we use thermometers when people are ill, parents can usually tell if their child has a temperature simply by touching his or her forehead. What is more, when you adjust the temperature of your bath by running more hot or cold water into the tub, your skin temperature receptors can pick up a temperature change of only 0.9 Fahrenheit degree (0.5 Celsius degree).

If your temperature sensors sense a rise or fall in your body temperature, your body responds. If you are too hot, you sweat. Your skin also turns pink as blood vessels near the surface of your skin open up to cool you. This brings more blood to the surface of the skin, where it releases heat energy. If you are too cold, your blood supply is directed away from the skin to the vital organs. You start shivering to generate heat. You also get goose bumps. Goose bumps raise the small hairs that cover your body. This is a way to trap an insulating layer of air near your skin and hold on to heat energy.

Complications

Measuring energy is harder than it might seem. Next time you are sipping a hot chocolate, think about all the energy that has been used to warm it up. One way of measuring this is to take the temperature of the drink. If it is at 120°F (49°C) you know it contains more energy than if it was only at 100°F (38°C). There is more to it than this, though. What size is your cup? It takes more energy to heat a big cup of hot chocolate up to 120°F (49°C) than a small cup.

How much energy?

Now think about a swimming pool. The water in a pool is usually about 86°F (30 °C), which is not hot. But there is a huge amount of water in a swimming pool, so a huge amount of energy is needed to heat it up. It is important to remember that the amount of heat energy in an object cannot be measured simply by measuring its temperature.

Working hard
Heating the water in a swimming pool to only 86°F (30 °C) uses much more energy than heating a pot of water to 212°F (100 °C).

Doing work

One of the important facts about energy is that it is used for doing work. That work might be heating things up or moving things around. When you visit a department store, the things you want to buy may be on one of the higher floors. You have two choices on how to get there. You might take the stairs, or you might use the elevator. Moving your body mass against the force of gravity for a distance of 50 feet (15 m) takes a lot of energy. This can be measured by multiplying your weight in newtons by the distance it is lifted in meters. The elevator will have done exactly the same amount of work to lift you as your legs, because it will have raised your mass up 50 feet (15 m). (For the sake of this explanation we ignore the weight of the elevator and the work that has to be done to raise it.) The amount of energy used will be the same, but there is one big difference: the elevator probably will have moved you upward faster than your legs could have.

Another important measurement when considering energy is power, the rate at which energy is transferred from one place to another, or at which work is done. Although the elevator and your legs will have done the same amount of work in moving you up, the elevator motor has used more power than your leg muscles if it has lifted you up in a shorter time.

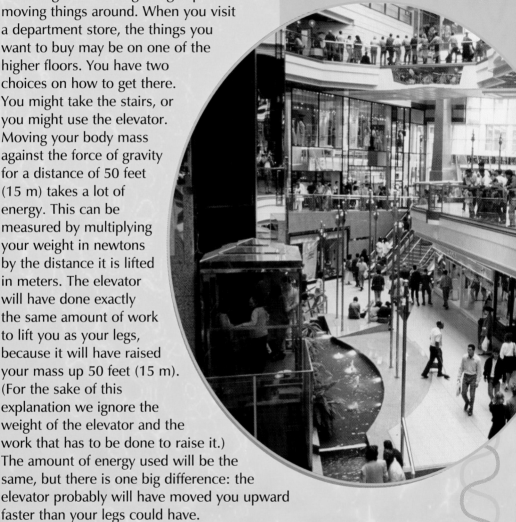

Taking the strain
Moving upward feels easier in an elevator because our legs do not have to provide the power to lift our body weight.

Kinetic Energy

All forms of energy can be divided into two basic types. The energy of motion is called kinetic energy, while stored energy is called potential energy. Kinetic energy involves any kind of motion. It can be you running, or the motion of molecules, atoms, and electrons that are too tiny for us to see but that affect us all the time.

Energy in motion

The simplest form of kinetic energy to understand is the energy of large moving objects. As you move around, you have kinetic energy. You feel its impact if someone runs into you. The amount of energy a moving object has depends on its mass and its speed. A heavy person running at the same speed as a light person will have more kinetic energy. A light person running really fast may have as much kinetic energy as, or more than, a heavy person moving slowly.

Kinetic energy explains why it is so important for cars to travel slowly in crowded areas. Kinetic energy increases at the same rate as the square of the speed. This means that a speed increase of just a few miles or kilometers per hour increases the kinetic energy of the vehicle enormously. This means the car is more likely to cause severe injuries or death if it hits anyone. Lowering your speed quickly reduces the kinetic energy of the car.

Deadly speed
A speed reduction of only 10 miles (16 km) per hour can mean that a person is only badly shaken rather than killed in a crash.

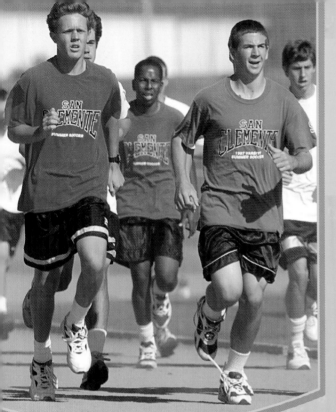

Warmed up
When you run, your body heat increases sharply, showing the link between movement and heat energy!

Moving things together

Rub your hands together briskly. What do you notice? They should feel warmer. When any two things move against each other they get hotter as a result of friction. If you touch car tires after a trip, they may feel hot. We use oil in vehicle engines to prevent the working parts from rubbing directly against each other. This prevents them from getting so hot that they expand and stick together. We heat our homes and our bath water, and we cook. All of these things involve heat energy. But what is heat energy?

To understand heat energy, we have to understand matter. Everything is made up of tiny particles (atoms and molecules) that we cannot see. These particles are all moving. This movement produces heat energy, so heat energy is kinetic energy. When an object is hot, its atoms and molecules are said to be excited—that is, they contain high energy and are moving rapidly.

Imagine some balloons hung outside. If the day is hot, the balloons get bigger and might burst, but if they are left out all night they get cold and become smaller and shrunken. Why? When particles have high levels of energy and are moving around rapidly, they take up more space. This is why things expand (grow bigger) when they are hot. When the atoms and molecules slow down as they cool, they take up less space, so things grow smaller (contract) as they cool down.

Kinetic Energy as Heat

Imagine a bar of chocolate that has been left inside a hot car for a few hours. The gooey, melted result shows us clearly that heat energy can travel. Cats know this; if there is a particularly warm spot in a house, a cat will certainly find it and enjoy the transfer of heat energy from the warm spot to itself.

Conduction

Have you ever left a metal spoon in a saucepan on the stove, and then gone back to stir the food? Do not try it—the spoon will be painfully hot! Heat energy flows from an area of high temperature to one with a lower temperature. In solids this is called conduction. It happens when energy is transferred from one atom or molecule to another touching it. Conduction is partly to blame for the fact that your cup of cocoa cools down. The heat energy does not disappear. It is transferred into the cup and the air. Heat energy travels more easily through some materials, such as metals, than it does through others, such as glass. Metals are known as good conductors of heat, while glass is a poor conductor.

Very hot
Heat energy travels, which is why sitting around a campfire to get warm works so well.

Vacuum bottles

To keep things hot, we have to prevent heat loss by conduction, convection, and radiation. The vacuum bottle is designed to minimize the transfer of heat energy in or out. Factors that work to prevent heat loss also prevent heat gain. So vacuum bottles are just as good at keeping things cold as keeping things hot—ideal for ice tea as well as hot cocoa on picnics!

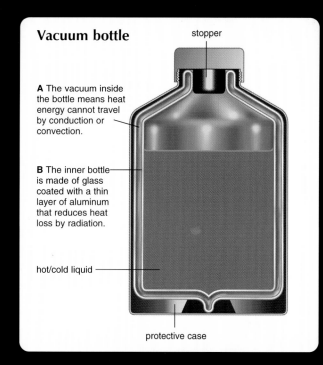

Vacuum bottle

stopper

A The vacuum inside the bottle means heat energy cannot travel by conduction or convection.

B The inner bottle is made of glass coated with a thin layer of aluminum that reduces heat loss by radiation.

hot/cold liquid

protective case

Convection

The principle of heat energy being transferred from a hotter to a colder area also applies to fluids—liquids and gases. This usually happens when movement—known as a convection current—occurs in the fluid. As the fluid grows warmer near a source of heat, it expands, becoming less dense, and so rises through the cooler (denser) fluid. It is replaced by cooler fluid, which is heated in its turn. Convection currents affect everyday actions. For example, when you put ice cubes in a drink, the cooled liquid sinks and is replaced by slightly warmer liquid. The warmer liquid in turn comes into contact with the cold ice and sinks.

Radiation

Everything gives off electromagnetic radiation of many different wavelengths, some of which we can see as visible light. The hotter an object is, the more long-wavelength infrared radiation it gives off. So when something is really hot, it glows red. A fire glows red as it provides us with heat. We can use this heat to grill food.

Kinetic Energy as Electricity

Most of us never think about electrical energy. We flick light switches or grab the remote without ever wondering what it really is, this electricity we rely on. Electrical energy is one of the most useful forms of energy because it can easily be transferred into other types of energy, such as heat, light, or movement. Read more about this on pages 34 and 35.

Inside atoms

Just like heat energy, electrical energy is actually a form of kinetic energy. In the case of electricity, however, it is not whole atoms and molecules that are moving, but electrons. No one can actually see atoms, so what we know about their structure is a scientific model. A model is a picture based on all the different evidence we have that attempts to explain the way atoms behave. The current model of an atom has a positively charged central nucleus containing particles called neutrons (heavy neutral particles) and protons (heavy positively charged particles) held together by very strong forces. Moving incredibly quickly around the nucleus is a cloud of negatively charged electrons (very light particles with a negative charge). The atom is electrically neutral because the number of protons and electrons is always exactly equal, and in most cases very stable.

In most atoms the electrons circle the nucleus, held close by the protons' positive charges. Sometimes, however—for instance in metals—the electrons are freed from this structure, so they can move around. It is this movement of electrons, or flow of charge, that we call electricity.

To give you an idea of how many electrons are involved in the electricity we use every day, it takes an estimated 6.28 billion billion electrons to keep a small flashlight lit for just one second!

Supplying the need

Huge quantities of electricity can be moved from place to place quite simply in metal wires. The wires on the huge overhead pylons of the National Grid can carry very much more electrical energy than the wires in your home—up to 400,000 volts compared with 120 volts in your home. Transformers are used to ensure that the electricity arriving at your wall sockets is exactly the right voltage to allow your appliances to work safely.

High wires

Electricity pylons carry huge amounts of electrical energy and distribute it all over the country.

Conductors and insulators

Materials through which electricity can flow are known as conductors. The human body is quite a good conductor of electricity. This is why we have to be so careful when we deal with it. Our heartbeat and many other body functions are controlled by electrical impulses. So if a big electric shock passes through our body, it is likely to interrupt these vital functions. In short, electric shocks can kill!

Fortunately many other materials, such as wood, rubber, and plastic, do not have charged particles that can move. These materials cannot conduct electricity. These materials are known as insulators, and we use them to protect us from electric shocks. This is why electric wires are made of copper in the middle—to conduct the electricity—with a plastic coating on the outside to provide insulation from the current inside.

Electricity in Nature

The electricity we use is controlled electricity. We make it, we send it through the system, and we use it when we want it. However, electricity turns up in other places in our lives—where we cannot always control it with a switch!

Static electricity

Have you ever had a tiny electric shock when you step onto an escalator or out of a car? Have you ever rubbed a balloon on your sweater and stuck it to the wall? If so, you have experienced static electricity. The electricity we have looked at so far involves a flow of charge, but static electricity is different. It is a buildup of charge in one place—that is, it is static (still). Electrons are rubbed off one material and build up on another. The amount of charge increases until the difference between the negative and positive charges on the two materials (the potential difference) becomes so big that the electrons flow back to where they came from. This produces a small spark and an electric shock for anyone who happens to be in the way.

Thunder and lightning
Electrical storms are awe inspiring and involve huge amounts of electrical energy.

Static electricity around us

Static electricity builds up around us in everyday activities. Stroking a pet or combing your hair can cause enough static electricity to build up to have visible effects. Your hair may stand on end as the charged strands repel one another, or the cat might run off as a spark jumps!

Benjamin Franklin

In June 1752, American scientist Benjamin Franklin carried out an incredibly dangerous experiment. He flew a kite into a thundercloud to prove that lightning is electricity. He tied a key to the end of the kite's string. Then he saw and felt a spark jump from the key to his finger, showing that electricity was involved. He was incredibly lucky. If lightning had struck the kite, Franklin would almost certainly have been killed!

Using static electricity

Static electricity can be useful. Photocopiers and laser printers use a light-sensitive drum that develops different areas of static charge depending on the amount of light falling on it. Particles of toner are attracted to the static charge and then transferred to the paper to produce an image.

However, static electricity can also cause problems. Static sparks can cause explosions in fuel tanks, so great care has to be taken when delivering fuel to gas stations and refueling aircraft.

Lightning strikes

Some people are terrified of thunderstorms. Others find them exciting and enjoy watching one of nature's most dramatic displays. Whatever your view, thunderstorms are probably the most spectacular example of static electricity we can see.

In storm clouds, ice particles and water drops caught in swirling air currents tumble against each other, losing and gaining electrons and becoming charged with static electricity. The top of the cloud becomes positively charged, and the bottom negatively charged. If the charges in the cloud build up enough, they force a path to the ground through the air and discharge as a lightning flash. The electrical energy is changed into light, heat, and sound.

The temperature of a lightning strike is up to 54,000°F (30,000°C)—more than three times as hot as the surface of the Sun! The surrounding air heats up and expands so quickly that it travels faster than the speed of sound, breaking the sound barrier and causing a sonic boom—thunder!

Where's the storm?

A lightning bolt and clap of thunder begin at the same time. Sound travels at about 1,115 feet (340 m) per second. Light goes almost a million times faster! Count the seconds between flash and boom, and divide by three—the storm is that many kilometers away.

Kinetic Energy as Sound

Sit very quietly and listen hard. What can you hear? Voices, a clock ticking, music, traffic—whatever you hear, you are detecting sound. We live in a world full of sound, all caused when objects move quickly back and forth, or vibrate.

Speed of sound

English clergyman William Derham measured the speed of sound fairly accurately in 1708. He stood on top of a church and watched a cannon being fired 12 miles (19 km) away. Then he measured the time that passed before he heard the boom.

Sound waves

When a guitar string is plucked, the vibrations push rapidly backward and forward on the air around it, making the air particles collide. As they collide, energy is passed from one to another as a traveling pressure wave. Because sound is made up of pressure waves, it has to travel through a medium, such as air, water, or metal. Sound cannot travel through a vacuum.

We can feel sound vibrations as they are made. Press gently on your voice box—the lump on the front of your throat—as you speak. You can feel the vibrations it produces.

When you strike a drum, the skin is pushed in as you hit it, then moves out again. It flexes backward and forward very quickly, pushing on the air molecules around it and making the air pressure fall and then rise. These pressure changes are then passed on through the air.

This movement is a form of kinetic energy, and we call it sound. Sound waves are measured in hertz (Hz). 1 hertz equals one vibration per second. The normal range of hearing for a young person is 20 to 20,000 Hz.

Did you know?

Fishers in trawlers use sound waves to find schools of fish. The sound bounces back off the fish, and the fishers cast their nets.

A sound's loudness depends on the amount of energy carried in the sound waves. Big vibrations have big energy and produce loud sounds—sonic booms. The shock waves from explosions can cause us physical damage, from burst eardrums to damaged internal organs.

Sound speeds in different materials

Sound passes through solids and liquids faster than through air because solids and liquids are denser and so the vibrations move faster from one particle to another.

Material	Speed of sound traveling through
steel	19,800 feet (6,000 m) per sec
water	4,950 feet (1,500 m) per sec
air	1,125 f (343 m)/sec at 68°F (20 °C) & sea level

Using sound energy

We use sound all the time to communicate. We have developed many ways to communicate over greater distances. We do this by changing sound energy into electrical signals. These signals can travel thousands of miles or kilometers before being changed back into sound energy. But we use sound in other ways as well. In a technique called ultrasound scanning, sounds above 20,000 Hz are used to create images of the insides of solid objects. The ultrasound passes through the object and bounces back, or echoes. A computer turns the echoes into pictures on a screen.

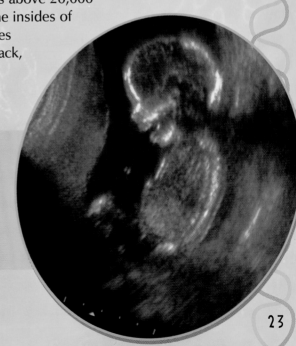

Bouncing echoes
Doctors use ultrasound scanning to see inside our bodies. For example, they can use it to look at babies before they are born to make sure they are developing normally.

23

Kinetic Energy as Light

Light energy illuminates our lives. Light energy from the Sun not only enables us to see, it enables us to exist. Plants use light energy—around 10^{19} kilojoules per year—to convert carbon dioxide and water into sugar and oxygen. In this process they provide us with the food we need to eat and the oxygen we need to breathe! So light energy is of vital importance to our everyday life on Earth.

What is light?

Light is a form of energy that travels in waves. Light waves can travel through a vacuum. This is why light from objects millions of miles away in space can reach Earth. Another important property of light becomes obvious when you use a flashlight. If you are using a flashlight to find your way around in the dark, you cannot shine your flashlight beam around corners. This is because light rays always travel in straight lines. They can be reflected—that is, they can change direction as they bounce off a solid object. Or they can be refracted—change direction and speed as they pass through different materials.

We know kinetic energy involves motion. So how fast does light travel? The most accurate measurements put the speed of light at 186,282 miles (299,792 km) per second. That really is impressive—nothing in the entire known universe travels faster!

Big lamp
The amount of light energy produced by the Sun is huge—around 10^{31} (100,000,000,000, 000,000,000,000,000, 000,000) kilojoules every year! It provides the energy for all food production on Earth.

Different wavelengths, different speeds

The light that we see is known as white light, or visible light. It is actually made up of different colored light rays combined together. White light can be split up into its different colors by passing it through a special piece of glass called a prism, which separates all the different colors into a spectrum. Each color of light has a different wavelength—red light has the longest wavelength and violet light the shortest—and they travel at different speeds. So each color is refracted by a different amount and they bend at different angles. Red bends the least and violet the most. The wavelength order of the colors is red, orange, yellow, green, blue, indigo, and violet. In a rainbow, each tiny droplet of water acts as a prism, splitting the sunlight into the spectrum that we see curving across the sky.

More than colors

The colors of light that we can see belong to a much larger family of waves, most of which we cannot see—the electromagnetic spectrum. In addition to visible light, the electromagnetic spectrum includes radio waves, microwaves, infrared light, ultraviolet light, X rays, and gamma rays. The electromagnetic spectrum touches almost everything in our lives, from household appliances to life-saving medical treatments.

Easy peas
Microwave ovens make heating food quick and easy using kinetic energy.

Microwave ovens

The microwave is an especially useful applicance because it heats food up so fast. The way it works shows the link between the motion of atoms and molecules and heat energy. A microwave oven produces electromagnetic waves, called microwaves, which are absorbed by water, fat, and sugar molecules in the food. As they absorb the microwaves, the molecules become excited and move around rapidly. The food gets hot!

Potential Energy

Most forms of kinetic energy are obvious. You can hear sounds, see things moving, and feel the impact if something collides with you. Other types of energy are less obvious. Most of this hidden energy is what we call potential energy. It is stored energy, available for use when we need it.

Energy up high

Lift a ball over your head. You had to use energy for this, and this energy was transferred to the ball. While it is up in the air, it contains gravitational potential energy. It is called this because the energy has been given to it by moving it against gravity. Once you let go of it, that potential energy is changed into motion, or kinetic energy, as the ball falls to the ground. Anything lifted above Earth's surface has gravitational potential energy and will, given the opportunity, transfer that energy into kinetic energy by falling back down to Earth.

Power and beauty
A waterfall is one of the most dramatic of all natural examples of gravitational potential energy changed into kinetic energy.

Picture yourself riding your bicycle up a hill. When you get to the top of the hill, you have gravitational potential energy. That energy can be changed into motion as you coast all the way down again! You can enjoy the ride without having to do any work.

Potential energy in nature

Nature has some amazing examples of gravitational potential energy. Imagine walking out in the countryside and finding a waterfall. Stand at the top and listen to the roar of the water as it tumbles over the falls. Look at the movement of the water and the rainbows dancing in the spray as tons of water transfer the gravitational potential energy in the pool at the top into kinetic and sound energy as the water plunges to the rocks below.

Elastic energy and springy springs

Have you ever used a trampoline, or just bounced on your bed? These activities depend on another sort of potential energy—elastic potential energy. This is the energy stored in something because of a change in its shape. When a spring or an elastic band is stretched, energy is stored in the material. When the stretch is released, the stored energy is transferred and is usually used to produce movement—bouncing you up into the air from the trampoline, for example!

Elastic energy is important in wind-up clocks and toys. In such devices, a key is used to wind up a metal spring. The energy stored in the spring is then transferred slowly into the movement of the hands of a clock or the parts of a toy. In the past, all clocks ran this way. Today some clocks still need regular winding, but most others rely instead on the chemical potential energy of batteries. We also use the elastic potential energy of springs—in mattresses and in the suspension systems in vehicles.

Using elastic energy

A great example of the use of elastic energy is the pole vault. A pole vaulter runs and plants the pole, bending it way down before taking off. The elastic potential energy stored in the bent pole is used to lift the vaulter 15 to 20 feet (4.5 to 6 m) up. At the top of the vault, the pole is dropped. The vaulter has plenty of gravitational potential energy. This energy is quickly transferred back into motion energy in the fall back to the ground.

Chemical Potential Energy

Most of us have used battery-operated toys and gadgets—for example, flashlights, personal stereos, and game consoles. But a video game does not work in its packaging, and an empty flashlight is no help to see in the dark. Put batteries in and, as if by magic, the graphics appear on the screen and a beam of light shines out from the flashlight. But it is not magic that starts things working. The changes are brought about as the stored chemical potential energy in the batteries is changed into useful electrical, light, and sound energy.

What is chemical potential energy?

To understand what chemical potential energy is, we have to look once more into the sub-microscopic world of atoms, molecules, and electrons.

An atom is made up of a nucleus surrounded by electrons. Atoms join to form molecules by making chemical bonds. The important thing about chemical bonds is that energy is needed to break them, and energy is released when new bonds are formed.

Did you know?

In 1938 an archaeologist digging near Baghdad, Iraq, found some little jars. Inside were iron rods surrounded by copper cylinders. Scientists think these jars may have been batteries. Craftworkers possibly used them to apply gold coatings to silver jewelry. They are 2,000 years old.

Batteries contain chemicals that act as an energy supply. Chemical reactions take place inside the battery and new bonds are formed. In this process, energy is released and is changed into electrical energy, which can then be put to many uses, such as operating games and flashlights.

The right battery for the job

The amount of chemical potential energy in a battery depends on several things. One is the chemical combination in the battery. Silver-zinc batteries can provide more energy than alkaline batteries of the same size. But silver-zinc batteries cost a lot more, so our everyday batteries are alkaline.

Inventing batteries

Italian scientist Alessandro Volta invented the first battery in 1799. He used a pile of copper and zinc discs. These discs were separated by cardboard discs soaked in salt water. A wire came out of the top and the bottom. The problem with this pile was that the wet cardboard kept drying out! A Frenchman named Georges Leclanché invented the modern battery in 1865.

Another factor is the size of the battery. Compare the size of the battery in a car to the size of a battery in a personal stereo or a watch! The car battery contains far more chemical potential energy—but it is bulky and very heavy. The type of battery you use depends on both the amount of energy you need and the situation you need it in. Devices such as watches and heart pacemakers are powered by tiny batteries, while huge batteries are needed for juggernauts and tanks.

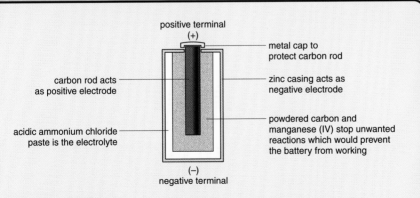

positive terminal
(+)

metal cap to protect carbon rod

carbon rod acts as positive electrode

zinc casing acts as negative electrode

acidic ammonium chloride paste is the electrolyte

powdered carbon and manganese (IV) stop unwanted reactions which would prevent the battery from working

(−)
negative terminal

Battery revealed

*The inside of one type of battery—the chemicals inside the battery are **corrosive** and so are contained within the outer case.*

Pops, Crackles, and Big Bangs

Matches are an amazing invention. We take them for granted, yet the little blob on the top of each match saves so much time and effort. Striking a match involves friction. Motion energy is changed into heat energy, and that heat triggers a reaction in the chemicals on the head of the match. This leads to a useful, controlled flame. Chemical potential energy is used to produce heat and light.

Making it easy
Matches give us a form of chemical potential energy so we can have fire wherever and whenever we want.

Explosions

Some people use party poppers for celebrations. The bang when you pull the string on your party popper and the energy that shoots the streamers up into the air also come from the chemical potential energy stored in the chemicals inside the popper. The explosions we see in movies or in fireworks displays are also caused by chemical potential energy. The explosive chemicals are relatively safe to handle. They can be positioned in a warhead on a missile, or in the fireworks before a display, and do not explode. Once a small amount of heat or electrical energy is added to them, however, there is a massive chemical reaction that gives out huge quantities of energy. Enormous amounts of chemical potential energy are changed into light, heat, sound, and motion in the form of an explosion.

The potential in gasoline

One form of chemical potential energy that most of us use every day is the potential energy in fuels. When gas or diesel fuel is burned in air, as in a car engine, the potential energy is released and changed into motion energy, heat, and sound. This chemical potential energy is used to move millions of vehicles on our roads every day.

Food for thought

Most of what we do with our bodies needs energy. That energy is supplied by the chemical potential energy in the chemical bonds of our food. The main types of food molecules that we eat are proteins, carbohydrates, and fats. These three contain different numbers and types of chemical bonds. As our bodies break down our food, we release the potential chemical energy and convert it into other forms of chemical energy that are easily used by our cells.

We cannot digest some of the chemicals we eat, such as the cellulose in plant material. So we cannot release their chemical potential energy. Other substances, particularly carbohydrates, are easily broken down to release usable energy. So different foods contain different amounts of available energy. This is why some foods are more fattening than others. If we eat too much food with plenty of available energy, we will take in more energy than we need. Our body will use the excess to store potential energy in the form of fat.

Dig in!
We do not usually think of a plate of food as chemical potential energy, but that's exactly what it is.

Nuclear Energy

Many forms of energy, such as light, heat, and sound, are obvious in our everyday lives. One form of energy, though, is present everywhere, yet we are largely unaware of it. That is the energy present in every atom.

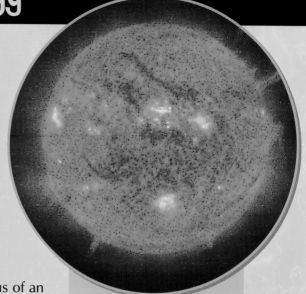

Inside atoms

The forces inside the nucleus of an atom are very powerful, and the energy released when they are broken is enormous. Nuclear reactions and nuclear energy are familiar terms to most of us. But we do not always recognize just how much we rely on them.

Our life giver
The Sun lights and warms our world. It is the source of energy for most life on our planet.

The nuclear Sun

The Sun, which is the main energy source for Earth, is basically a nuclear reactor. It is a huge ball of gas—mainly hydrogen with some helium. Nuclear reactions are always taking place within it. These reactions release the energy stored in the nuclei of the atoms. This energy is changed mainly into light and heat. Scientists estimate the temperature at the center of the Sun is about 52,200,000°F (14,000,000 °C). This means that an astonishing amount of energy is involved.

The reactions that power the Sun are known as nuclear fusion reactions. In these, the nuclei of hydrogen atoms collide and join, or fuse. This forms helium atoms and large amounts of energy. Scientists have spent years searching for ways to use this reaction to produce usable energy here on Earth, but so far they have been unsuccessful.

Nuclear fission

Another type of nuclear reaction, called nuclear fission, releases a huge amount of energy. If a large nucleus that is already slightly unstable (for instance, the nucleus of a uranium atom) is hit by a neutron, it may split into two smaller, stable nuclei. The amount of energy produced by the nuclear fission of a piece of uranium with a volume of 0.06 cubic inch (1 cm^3) is the same as we could produce from a pile of coal with a volume of 26,154,000 cubic inches (42,875,000 cm^3).

We have managed to harness this reaction more successfully than nuclear fusion. Nuclear fission reactions are used to provide the energy for a number of electricity-generating power plants. Quite a few of us get the energy we use in our homes every day indirectly from nuclear energy.

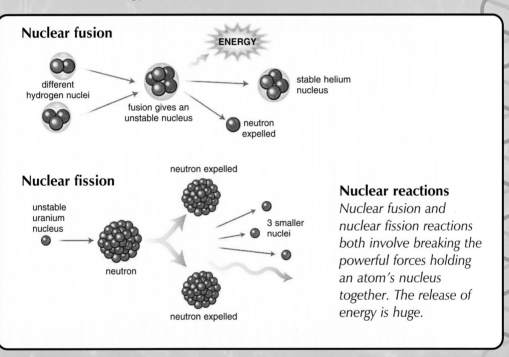

Nuclear fusion

ENERGY

different hydrogen nuclei

fusion gives an unstable nucleus

neutron expelled

stable helium nucleus

Nuclear fission

neutron expelled

unstable uranium nucleus

neutron

3 smaller nuclei

neutron expelled

Nuclear reactions
Nuclear fusion and nuclear fission reactions both involve breaking the powerful forces holding an atom's nucleus together. The release of energy is huge.

There is another use of the energy produced during nuclear reactions. This is in the production of atomic bombs and other nuclear weapons of mass destruction. This does not affect us directly in our everyday lives. But the threat of nuclear war in the world is a shadow over us all the time.

As you can see, potential energy comes in many shapes and forms and is often invisible and unnoticed. In spite of this, potential energy is as important for the maintenance of everyday life as any of the more obvious and spectacular forms of kinetic energy we looked at earlier.

Energy Transfers

Go for a walk on a wintry day and your fingers, toes, nose, and ears will soon feel chilly. Lie on a sunny beach in the summer and the opposite will happen. The Sun's heat will warm you. Turn on a light switch and the room is illuminated. Eat a meal and then play sports and you have the energy to keep going for a long time. These things all involve energy transfers. A striking thing about energy is the way transferring it lets us to do something useful.

Faraday and Henry

In 1831 British scientist Michael Faraday developed the first dynamo, and he managed to produce electricity! Joseph Henry was doing similar work in the United States. Faraday published his results first. So he gets credit for inventing the dynamo. After discovering how to generate electricity,however, Faraday lost interest in the subject. Henry, on the other hand, was a practical man. He went on to develop ways of generating electricity on a large enough scale to be really useful.

Driving with energy

Let's look again at the cars that play such an important role in our lives. We fill them with gasoline, a source of chemical potential energy. When we turn on the engine, the gasoline is burned in air to release its chemical potential energy. This potential energy is changed into two types of useful energy— motion energy (speeding up the car) and electrical energy (charging the battery, operating the lights). It also produces two types of wasted energy, heat and sound energy. The heat energy is not always wasted. In cold weather we use it to warm up the inside of the car.

Making electricity

Turn on the light. What is happening in terms of energy? Electrical energy flows through the wires and into the filament of the light bulb. As the current flows, the filament becomes hot and glows as electrical energy is changed to heat energy and light energy. We can see the light energy, and if we hold our hands near the light bulb, we can feel the heat energy.

Energy heroes
Michael Faraday (1791–1867) (left) and Joseph Henry (1797–1878) (right) discovered how to make electricity work for us.

We have seen that energy is never lost or destroyed. What happens to the heat and light energy once they leave the light bulb? They spread out though the universe to become part of the low-grade energy present everywhere in space. In almost every energy transfer, some energy is wasted. It is changed into a form of energy that is not useful to us and spreads out until it cannot be useful again.

But where does the electrical energy to light the bulb come from? Making electricity to fulfill all our needs is a big job, and every developed country has huge power plants to do just that. This is another example of the way we use energy transfers. Electricity can be produced when a magnet rotates in a coil of wire. In most power plants we burn fossil fuels—coal, natural gas, or oil—that are all rich sources of chemical potential energy. As the fuels are burned, heat energy is transferred to water. The water boils, producing steam. High-power jets of steam cause turbines to spin. More kinetic energy is in use as the turning of the turbines makes huge magnets turn within huge wire coils. This kinetic energy is then changed into electrical energy to supply our homes, hospitals, factories—everywhere where there is a need for electrical energy.

Food for Thought

Think about the food you have eaten today, both the kinds of food and how much of it you have had. Now think about all the food you have eaten during the last year. Recent statistics show that the average American teenager eats about 150 pounds (70 kg) of sugar and 220 pounds (100 kg) of meat each year. The food we take in, and the way we use it, make a fascinating story of everyday energy transfer.

An energy chain

All the energy we use in our bodies originally came from the Sun. Plants use energy from the Sun to make food and to grow, changing the light energy into chemical potential energy in the molecules that make up their cells. People and animals then eat the plants. They also eat animals that have eaten plants, so the chemical potential energy we take into our bodies all comes indirectly from the Sun. Plants use about 10^{19} kilojoules of solar energy each year to make sugars—a huge amount of chemical potential energy!

Food factories
Plants change light energy from the Sun into chemical potential energy. When we eat the plants, our bodies use this energy.

Mother power
A baby's whole body has been formed as a result of energy transfers in its mother's body.

What happens to our food?

The food you eat contains high levels of chemical potential energy, but often it is not in a form you can use right away. The large molecules of carbohydrates, proteins, and fats in food need to be broken down into much smaller molecules, such as a form of sugar called glucose. This happens during the process of digestion. The glucose then reacts with oxygen in your body cells to produce more easy-to-use chemical potential energy. Carbon dioxide and water are produced as waste products along with some heat energy. This process is called cellular respiration.

The chemical potential energy produced in cellular respiration is used for all kinds of things. It is used to create new you! Inside your body, you are always forming new cells used to make your body grow bigger, to replace cells that have worn out, and to repair damage when you hurt yourself. This chemical potential energy is also used for moving. Energy is transferred in your muscles to move you around. Yet more of the chemical potential energy of your food is changed into heat energy, to keep your body warm even when your surroundings are cold.

In addition to all the food you use in producing energy, there is much that you cannot digest. That material passes straight through your gut. If you think about the tons of food you have eaten during your lifetime, compared to the amount you now weigh, you will realize that the percentage of chemical potential energy in your food that is actually transferred into new you is very small indeed!

Avoiding Energy Transfers

In many regions, people have to heat their homes to keep warm when the weather is cold. Some of the heat they create to do this is lost. Because it is colder outside the house than inside, heat energy is transferred to the cooler area and wasted. How can we stop this from happening?

Preventing heat loss

Half of the energy used in Western Europe goes to heat and light the buildings where people live and work—homes, schools, hospitals, stores, offices, and factories. That is a huge amount of energy, especially when much of it is wasted. Heat energy that escapes by convection, conduction, and radiation from our buildings is lost to us. It spreads out to become part of the low-grade useless energy of the universe.

Modern houses are usually designed to reduce the transfer of heat energy from the inside to the outside. Older houses are less energy-efficient and can feel cold and drafty.

Hot house
This photo has been taken using an infrared camera. The white areas are where the most heat is escaping— mainly through the windows.

Reducing energy transfers from buildings

- Choose materials, such as concrete blocks, that are poor conductors of heat.
- Have a cavity between walls filled with insulating material such as plastic foam or beads.
- Windows with double, even triple glazing—two or three layers of glass with layers of air (a poor conductor of heat) between them—cuts heat loss.
- Smaller windows mean reduced heat energy loss.
- Insulating material under the roof reduces energy loss through the roof.

In some areas, the task is to cool down the inside temperature. Air-conditioning systems use electrical energy to move heat energy from the air inside a house or car to the outside. Air-conditioning systems work in the same way as a refrigerator. The features that help reduce heat loss from a warm house in cold weather help prevent heat from getting into a cool house when it is hot outside.

Insulating ourselves

Your body, just like your home, transfers heat energy to the world around it. You need to cover the areas that lose the most heat with layers of insulating materials that conduct heat poorly. Up to a third of your body heat is lost through your head. So in cold weather it is really important to cover your head to reduce heat energy transfers. Wear several layers of clothing to trap layers of insulating air. Gloves and warm socks help reduce heat loss from your hands and feet. Wearing the right clothes reduces the amount of heat energy you lose on a cold day.

For most of us, reducing heat energy transfers is simply a case of making life more comfortable. But for elderly people and people working, walking, or doing recreational activities in exposed areas, reducing heat loss can mean the difference between life and death from the cold.

Energy Resources

We have looked at many examples of the role energy plays in our everyday lives. Now, where does all that energy come from? There are a number of different answers, but one of the major sources of energy we use here on Earth is fossilized sunlight! To find out just how we manage to do that, read on.

Trees for energy

There is nothing like sitting around a log fire on a cold winter's evening. Burning wood is another way we use energy from the Sun. The chemical potential energy in the wood came from the sunlight energy transferred to the tree as it photosynthesized. When we burn the wood in air, the process of combustion releases that chemical potential energy and transfers it to heat and light energy in the flames.

While it is easy to see how energy from the Sun is transferred to our food and into our wood, it may come as more of a surprise to realize that the gasoline we pump into our cars also contains chemical potential energy transferred from the Sun. What is more, much of the electricity we use has also ultimately come from the Sun. How? To answer that question we need to travel back millions of years through the history of Earth, to the formation of fossil fuels.

Sunny energy
Whether we eat plants or plant-eating animals, the energy we eat has been transferred from the light energy of the Sun.

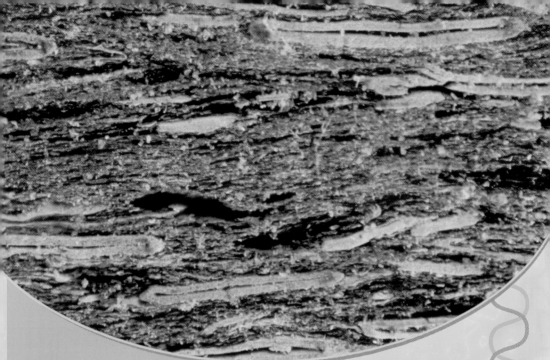

Ancient energy

In prehistoric times, the Earth was covered in lush vegetation. Many of the plants were giant tree-sized versions of todays ferns and brackens. Prehistoric plants relied on the Sun for food just as modern plants do, and they used the food they made to build up new plant material containing chemical potential energy.

When these huge plants died, layer upon layer of them built up. The plant remains were covered with sand and mud sediments, which over millions of years turned to rock. Often the dead plants rotted away, but sometimes they were simply crushed and covered. Over time, the plants became shiny black fossil material. People discovered this material millions of years later and called it coal.

Coal contains the concentrated chemical potential energy transferred from the Sun into those prehistoric plants. People have dug coal from the ground and used it as a source of heat and light energy for hundreds of years. Today its main use is as a fuel for producing electricity in power plant. The heat energy created when coal is burned in air is transferred to kinetic energy in turbines and then into electrical energy for people to use.

More Fossil Fuels

For many years coal was probably the best-known fossil fuel. Today, however, the fossil fuel most people think of first is oil. Crude oil is refined to provide people with fuels for cars, trucks, and aircraft. It also provides many of the chemicals used to make plastics and other everyday materials, and the fuel for many power plants.

Making oil

Crude oil is a thick, smelly black or brown sludge that is extracted from the ground in many parts of the world. It is one of the world's most valuable resources because of the tremendous amount of chemical potential energy it contains. Once again this energy originally came from the Sun.

Millions of years ago in the early seas lived huge numbers of tiny plantlike organisms called phytoplankton. They floated in the water and made food by capturing the energy of the Sun in the process of photosynthesis. These organisms were the food supply of huge colonies of other types of tiny animals known as zooplankton. Zooplankton in turn were the food of other small sea creatures, such as shrimps. When these tiny organisms died, their bodies sank to the bottom of the sea. Over millions of years, layers of sand and mud buried the dead organisms and formed sedimentary rocks. The action of heat and pressure turned the decayed remains of the organisms into crude oil, usually with a layer of natural gas on top. So, as with coal, the chemical potential energy in crude oil and natural gas came originally from the Sun. Our fossil fuels are really fossilized sunlight!

Black gold!
Crude oil is a concentrated source of chemical potential energy. Countries with large oil deposits depend on it for wealth and power.

Energy scores

Different types of energy resources contain different amounts of energy. We value fossil fuels so highly because they are a concentrated energy source. We can use a fairly small amount to produce a lot of usable energy. Fossil fuels are a much more efficient source of energy than plant material grown now, such as wood. We can see this from their relative energy values per gram: wood 20 kilojoules, coal 27 kilojoules, oil 42 kilojoules, and gas 55 kilojoules. Natural gas contains the most chemical potential energy, closely followed by oil. They are concentrated because huge numbers of dead organisms have been squashed together under great pressure to make them.

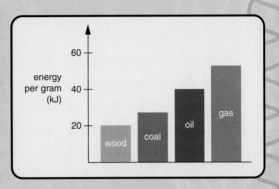

Global energy unit

When we look at the world's energy consumption, we do not think about grams of fuel! We talk about million tons of oil equivalent—in other words, the amount of energy in one million tons of oil. This unit is used by the energy industry throughout the world to make fair comparisons between different fuels. One ton of oil equivalent is about 40,000,000 kilojoules!

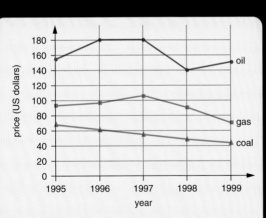

Fuel price graph
This graph shows changes in the price of oil, coal, and natural gas in the late 1990s, given in U.S. dollars per ton of oil equivalent.

Problems with Fossil Fuels

We have learned how people benefit from different forms of energy. There are, however, some negative factors to think about if we are to continue to have cheap energy at our fingertips for years to come.

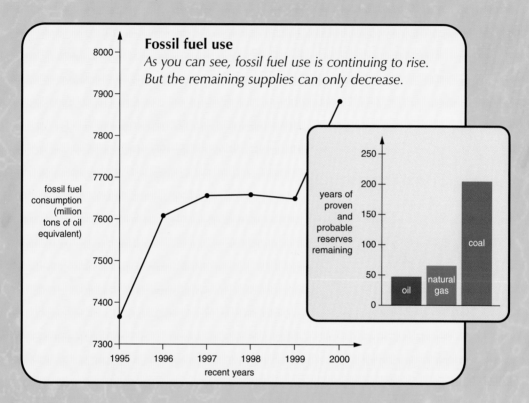

Fossil fuel use
As you can see, fossil fuel use is continuing to rise. But the remaining supplies can only decrease.

fossil fuel consumption (million tons of oil equivalent)

recent years

years of proven and probable reserves remaining

oil   natural gas   coal

If you read newspapers or magazines or watch current affairs programs on TV, you will know there are problems with our use of fossil fuels. One is that fossil fuels are just that—fossils, formed millions of years ago. The supply of fossil fuels—coal, oil, and natural gas—left for us to mine and drill is very limited.

A finite resource

People in the developing world use only a fraction of the energy used in developed countries. For example, North America uses about 1,500 million tons of oil equivalent of fossil fuels each year. In contrast, Central and South America together use only about 350 million tons of oil equivalent, and India uses only 280 million tons.

We cannot predict exactly when fossil fuels will be used up because new reserves are found from time to time. Also, the technology available to get every last bit of oil is improving. But it is clear that people must find other energy sources soon.

Polluting the planet, destroying our world

When fossil fuels burn, the energy released can work for people. However, some of this energy is wasted. More seriously, burning fossil fuels produce chemicals that damage the world. One of these chemicals is a gas called carbon dioxide. As the carbon dioxide content of the atmosphere increases, it forms an insulating layer that prevents the Earth from losing the Sun's heat by radiation. This is known as the greenhouse effect. Because of people's use of fossil fuels, carbon dioxide levels have been climbing for years. Some scientists believe that Earth's climate is warming up as a result. Global warming threatens the climate of the world. As the ice caps melt and sea levels rise, coastal areas may disappear under the sea, and some areas may become uninhabitable hot, dry deserts.

Coal and oil also give off other gases, such as sulfur dioxide and nitrogen oxides. These chemicals combine with water in the atmosphere to form acid rain and chemical smogs. These substances cause damage to the environment and to people's health. Acid rain has killed forests and lakes and damaged many buildings across Europe and the United States. Pollution from car fumes brings smog to cities, causing lung diseases such as asthma and bronchitis. No wonder scientists are seeking new sources of energy.

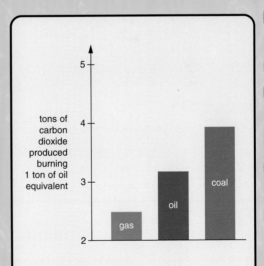

The downside of fossil fuels
High levels of carbon dioxide and the effects of acid rain and other fuel-related pollution threaten our everyday life and our health.

Energy in the Future

Looking at the harmful effects of using fossil fuels can make it seem like these problems will never be solved. But some people have already come up with useful substitutes for fossil fuels. More ideas are being developed as energy sources of the future.

New energy sources

What about now? What are some substitutes for coal, oil, and gas as fuels in our power plants? Nuclear energy, which you learned about on pages 32–33, is one familiar substitute for fossil fuels. Nuclear power is very promising as an energy source, but it also has many problems. Geothermal energy, which uses the natural heat under the Earth's surface, is a very effective energy source in areas where it is available, such as Iceland and some U.S. states.

Other new energy sources in use are often called renewable energy sources. Unlike fossil fuels, renewable energy sources can be used again and again and will not run out. They are also cleaner than burning fossil fuels. When you play a computer game or turn on the light, you could be using electricity from one of these cleaner resources.

Water power

Water in a river approaching a waterfall has huge potential energy. As water rushes downward, this potential energy is changed into kinetic energy. People have harnessed this energy in the form of hydroelectric power. Water collects in a reservoir, a large lake usually created when a river is dammed. The water is allowed to fall to a lower level through huge pipes. Its force is used to drive large turbines that make electricity. Hydroelectric power is clean and efficient. It is easy to control the amount of electricity made, and the power plants can be hidden underground or within the dam itself. The main problem is that building a dam can have a negative effect on the local environment. All over the world, many villages—up to a million people's homes—have disappeared under water as a result of hydroelectric projects. The water can also provide breeding grounds for malaria mosquitoes and affect farming in the surrounding area.

Wind power

People have been
using wind power for
centuries, to grind corn
in windmills. Now we have
wind farms to produce
electricity. Huge wind turbines are
put up in windy areas. As the wind drives
spinning blades, the kinetic energy is used to turn turbines and
create electricity. Wind power is virtually pollution-free, although
the blades can be noisy and sometimes interfere with radio signals.
The turbines also kill a lot of birds that fly into the blades. Some
people object to wind farms because they feel they spoil beautiful
countryside. Offshore wind farms will probably solve this problem
and generate even more electricity—it is usually windy out at sea!
But the high cost of building and maintaining offshore wind farms
must be considered.

Solar energy

So much energy from the Sun shines down on Earth that it would be
fantastic if we could use this neverending resource. We can do this in
several ways. A small example is a solar-powered calculator. A
photovoltaic, or solar, cell transfers the light energy from the Sun into
electrical energy to help with your math! The same thing on a bigger
scale can be used to create electricity or to heat a house. Solar energy
can also be used to heat up water in huge boilers, producing steam
that can be used to drive turbines and produce electricity.

Conserving Energy

Think about the future and how you imagine yourself in 20, 30, or 40 years. Whatever you hope to be, you will almost certainly want a nice home and a car, and to have plenty of readily available energy. One of the biggest problems people will face over the next 50 years is how to supply the energy everyone wants and needs without ruining the planet. People are facing a genuine energy crisis. Not everyone is taking it seriously or looking for solutions, but many people are working hard on the problem. They are taking two different approaches.

Energy efficiency

One approach to the energy crisis is to increase our energy efficiency. Switch a light on. One traditional light bulb shows clearly how much energy is wasted. The reason for this is that light bulbs are really bad at changing electrical energy into light energy. Only a tiny part of the electrical energy from the main supply ends up as light energy. Most of it becomes wasted heat energy. Today's low-energy light bulbs do a much better job, producing a bigger percentage of light and far less heat. Furthermore, they last longer and so save energy in their production as well.

Bright idea
One ordinary light bulb uses the same amount of energy as four energy-saving light bulbs.

48

Aluminum efficiency

Aluminum is extracted from its ore using electricity. Here are some facts about aluminum:

- In the last 50 years, the amount of electrical energy needed to produce aluminum has fallen by over a third.
- 54.1% of the electricity used to produce aluminum worldwide now comes from renewable hydroelectric power
- Modern cans are thinner and require 40 percent less aluminum.
- Recycling aluminum has become common. Making aluminum from recycled material takes only 5 percent of the energy needed to get the same amount from ore.

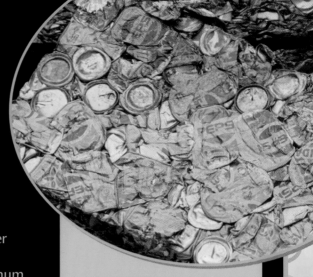

Reuse it or lose it
Recycling makes energy reserves last longer. Some countries recycle up to 80 percent of household waste.

It is not only light bulbs that can be made more efficient. There are efficiency developments in all sorts of areas. These include designing homes to hold in heat and designing cars that use less fuel. In some countries, such as the United States, where gasoline is less expensive, few people understand the importance of energy-efficient cars. But in many European countries, where gasoline is more expensive, fuel economy is an important selling point.

Recycling

Another important area is the recycling of materials. A lot of energy is needed to dig materials such as metals from the Earth. Much of this energy is wasted when people use metal produced once and then throw it away. From cars and computers to food packaging, people are working to make more things that can be recycled. Recycle your aluminum drink cans! Far less energy is used in recycling aluminum than in producing it from its original ore.

As people become more aware of the value of recycling and develop the technology to recycle more types of materials, much energy will be saved worldwide. If people conserve more energy, fossil fuel reserves will last longer. This will give people more time to develop effective new energy resources.

Winning with Waste

Nuclear, hydroelectric, and wind power are the main substitutes for fossil fuel energy in use at the moment. But the technology for harnessing other good energy sources is already being developed.

Waste matters

Biogas generators are allowing communities all over the world to produce methane gas, either to supply heat energy or to generate electricity.

Biological fuels are making an impact. In many less developed parts of the world small biogas generators are being used to produce energy for families or villages. We all have to get rid of body waste regularly, and plant-eating animals produce huge amounts of dung. Biogas generators are small units containing microorganisms that break down feces and food waste and produce methane gas. Methane is the same chemical as the natural gas found with crude oil. This gas burns fairly cleanly to provide heat energy for cooking, heating water, or producing electricity. This can happen on a larger scale in the developed world. People are working to develop the technology to produce biogas generators to be used with the garbage we produce every day in the preparation of our food.

Biofuels

Gasohol and biodiesel are cleaner than gasoline and diesel, and both will be made more widely available. Ethanol (the alcohol in alcoholic drinks) produced from sugarcane was first used as fuel for cars in South America. Now many U.S. states produce gasohol, a mixture of ethanol made from corn and ordinary gasoline. Gasohol burns more cleanly than pure gasoline, and it is a partly renewable resource.

Biodiesel is diesel fuel made from plants such as soybeans. It can be used in ordinary diesel vehicles and is a completely renewable resource. It just needs plenty of land and good growing conditions. In the future, genetic engineering may help by allowing scientists to develop high-yield biodiesel crops that grow faster in poor conditions.

Fuel cells: energy for the future

The energy produced in many spacecraft comes from fuel cells, which are devices similar to batteries. They make use of the stored potential energy in molecules to make electricity. Fuel cells (or hydrogen cells) are one of our most exciting prospects for future energy production. They are compact and clean. The water produced by fuel cells in the U.S. space station Skylab was used for washing and drinking.

If fuel cells take over the world's electrical energy production, people could use less fossil fuel and cut down on pollution. Several types of fuel cells are being developed. Some can be used for large-scale electricity production in power plants. Others could be used to power cars, light the home, or run portable gadgets. Electricity generated by the reaction between hydrogen gas and the oxygen in the air in fuel cells may be the main source of energy in years to come.

About the future, two things seem certain: The world's energy demands will continue to grow. And science and technology will allow people to meet those demands in an ever more environmentally friendly way.

Fuel cells: pros and con

Pros
- They can use the air around us.
- They have many uses and can generate energy at all levels.
- They are water-based, using the simple reaction between hydrogen and oxygen, producing water.

Con
- It is difficult to find a readily available supply of hydrogen.

Summary: Our Energetic Universe

Energy is the basis of everything. The whole universe, as well as your life, depends on it. People use energy in many different ways, from the chemical potential energy that keeps their cells working, to the burning of fossil fuels that powers their cars. People make use of energy transfers to provide exactly the energy they need in the right place at the right time.

World-friendly driving
The Shell oil company runs a yearly competition for the most fuel-efficient car. This car, made by Andy Green, finished fourth in 2002. It averaged 5,191 miles (8,352 km) per gallon.

Electrical energy is very important for the way of life in developed countries. Electricity provides heat, light, and all the different technologies people rely on to make their lives comfortable. But because of the environmental damage caused by burning fossil fuels, people need to think carefully about the way they use electrical energy and the ways they produce it.

Today's world energy crisis involves more than just electricity. More and more people all over the world own cars, and cars burn fossil fuels. Scientists are working both on new, cleaner energy sources and on ways of making people's energy use more efficient.

Energy is involved when we throw a ball into the air, and when water cascades over a waterfall. Light energy illuminates our days and our nights, while sound energy gives us information about the world and allows us to communicate quickly and easily. Chemical potential energy allows many things to happen exactly when we choose, such as turning on a flashlight or moving our legs to walk around. Energy means life—enjoy it!

52

Glossary

acid rain rain with high acid content as a result of pollution. Acid rain damages the environment

biodiesel form of diesel fuel made from the breakdown of plant oils

biofuels, biological fuels fuels made from the breakdown of biological material

biogas generators generators for making biogas from the decay of plant or animal waste in the absence of air

calibrate ensure that a measuring instrument gives accurate readings

calorie unit of heat energy, enough to raise 1 gram of water by 1 °C

calorimeter instrument for measuring the energy content of food

calorimetry method of measuring the energy content of food

cellulose complex carbohydrate found in plant cell walls

chemical bond force holding atoms together in a molecule or crystal

chemical potential energy energy held in a chemical bond that is released during reactions

coal carbon-based fuel made from the fossilized remains of prehistoric plants

conduction movement of heat or electricity through a substance

conductor substance through which heat or electricity can flow

convection transfer of heat through a fluid by currents within the fluid

corrosive slowly damaging by chemical reaction

developed countries wealthy nations that control the global economy

dynamo generator that changes mechanical energy into electrical energy

elastic potential energy energy stored in an elastic substance when it is stretched or compressed

electrons subatomic particles with a negative charge

energy capacity to do work

ethanol simple alcohol, C_2H_5OH

flex bend

fluid substance that can flow, such as a gas, vapor, or liquid

fossil fuel fuel formed over millions of years from the remains of animals or plants

friction force that affects surfaces in contact with each other, slowing down or preventing movement

fuel cell device that produces electricity by oxidizing a fuel

gamma rays type of electromagnetic radiation

genetic engineering directly changing or working with the genes of an organism to produce a desired trait, or characteristic

hydroelectric power electrical energy produced from the energy in moving water

insulator material that reduces the flow of heat, sound, or electricity, a poor conductor

kilojoule (kJ) unit of energy equal to 1,000 joules

kilowatt unit of power

kinetic energy energy associated with movement

mass amount of matter contained in a body

matter something with mass and volume that takes up space

million tons of oil equivalent amount of any fuel that contains the same amount of energy as a million tons of oil

negative charge electric charge of the type carried by electrons

neutron subatomic particle with no charge found in the nucleus of an atom

newton unit of force

nuclear fission reaction in which the nucleus of an atom splits into two smaller nuclei, releasing energy

nuclear fusion energy-releasing reaction in which two small, light nuclei fuse together to form a single heavier nucleus

nuclear reaction reaction involving the nucleus of an atom

photosynthesis process by which plants make food from carbon dioxide and water using energy from the Sun

positive charge electric charge of a type opposite of the charge carried by electrons

potential difference difference in energy between two parts of an electric circuit

potential energy energy that is stored in a system, for example, because of its position

power rate of energy transfer, measured in watts

proton heavy positively charged subatomic particle found in the nucleus of an atom

reflect bounce sound, light, or heat back from a surface

refraction bending of a beam of light as it passes from one material to another of different density, for example, from air to water

sonic boom extremely loud explosive sound produced when something goes faster than the speed of sound

static electricity electrical charge that builds up on an object as electrons are either rubbed off or deposited onto it

temperature measure of how cold or hot something is

thermometer instrument for measuring temperature

thermostat instrument for controlling temperature

transformer device that changes the voltage in an electrical system

turbine machine for producing power

ultrasound sound with a frequency higher than can be picked up by the human ear

vacuum space containing nothing

voltage electromotive force or potential difference expressed in volts

watt unit of power

work transfer of energy from one system to another

X ray type of short-wavelength electromagnetic wave that can pass through many materials, used to obtain photographs of the inside of the body and for other purposes

Further Reading

Books

Arnold, Nick. *Horrible Science: Killer Energy*. New York: Scholastic, 1999.

The Dorling Kindersley Science Encyclopedia. New York: Dorling Kindersley, 1999.

Hawkes, Nigel. *Focus on Science: Heat and Energy*. New York: Franklin Watts, 2003.

Parker, Steve. *Green Files: Future Power*. Chicago: Heinemann Library, 2003.

Searle, Bobby, and Catherine Ward. *Fascinating Science Projects: Heat and Energy*. New York: Franklin Watts, 2002.

Sneddon, Robert. "Energy for Life" series. Chicago: Heinemann Library, 2003.

Index